Level 3 Advanced Bookkeeping

Practice Assessment

By

Teresa Clarke FMAAT

This practice assessment has been written and designed to be as similar as possible to the real AAT Level 3 Advanced Bookkeeping exam. It includes a similar mark scheme so you can work out your percentage pass rate too.

Answers are shown on page 20 onwards.

A marks sheet is included at the back of this assessment for you to record your marks.

You need 70% to pass this exam.

NOTE
Unlike other practice assessments, I have shown workings and given explanations to help you understand where the answers have come from. This will help you to understand any errors you make.

Time allowed – 2 hours

Task 1 (21 marks)

This task is about non-current assets.

You are working on the accounting records of TC Enterprises for the year ended 31 March 2021.

You can ignore VAT in this task.

The following is an extract from a purchase invoice for some office equipment purchased by TC Enterprises.

Alphabeta Office Supplies Ltd 16 The Terrace Northport		30 September 2020
To: TC Enterprises			
Item	Details	Total cost £
Corner desk unit	DK101A	560.00
Assembly cost	DK101A	60.00
Manager's chair	MC20B	220.00
Net total		840.00

Payment was made by bank transfer on 30 September 2020.

The following relates to the sale of a vehicle.

Item description	Transport lorry ID no. TPL12
Date of sale	1 June 2020
Selling price	£8,000

The business has a policy of capitalising equipment over £500.

Vehicles are depreciated at 20% diminishing balance. This depreciation is charged in the year of acquisition but none in the year of disposal.

Office equipment is depreciated at 10% straight line assuming no residual value and charged in equal instalments for each month the asset is owned.

a) For the year ended 31 March 2021, record the following in the extract from the non-current assets register below. (18 marks)

Any acquisition of new equipment.
Any disposals of equipment.
Depreciation.

Note. Not every cell will require an answer. Round your answers to the nearest whole pound. Use the date format DD/MM/YY for your answers.

Extract from the non-current assets register.

Description	Acquisition date	Cost £	Depreciation charges £	Carrying amount £	Funding method	Disposal proceeds £	Disposal date
Office equipment							
Meeting table	01/06/19	1,200			Bank		
Year-end 31/03/20			100	1,100			
Year-end 31/03/21							
Year-end 31/03/21							
Vehicles							
Delivery van DV62	01/04/18	30,000			Loan		
Year-end 31/03/19			6,000	24,000			
Year-end 31/03/20			4,800	19,200			
Year-end 31/03/21							
Transport lorry TPL12	01/04/18	80,000			Credit		
Year-end 31/03/19			16,000	64,000			
Year-end 31/03/20			12,800	51,200			
Year-end 31/03/21							

b) The asset register should be checked against a physical count of assets at the end of the year. (3 marks)

True	
False	

Task 2 (17 marks)

This task is about ledger accounting for non-current assets.

You are working on the accounting records of a business with the year end of 31 March 2021.

VAT can be ignored.

A new vehicle has been acquired and it is expected to have a useful life of 5 years.

The cost was £26,000 and this was paid from the bank.

The business plans to sell the vehicle after 5 years when it is expected to have a residual value of £5,000.

Vehicles are depreciated using the straight-line method with a full year's depreciation in the year of acquisition and none in the year of disposal.

Depreciation has already been entered in the accounting records for other vehicles.

a) (12 marks) Calculate the depreciation charge for the new vehicle.

£

Make entries for the acquisition of the new vehicle and the depreciation charge of the new vehicle.

Balance off the accounts clearly showing the amount to be transferred to the Statement of Profit or Loss or carried down.

Vehicles at cost

Dr	£	Cr	£
Balance b/d	260,000		

Depreciation charges

Dr	£	Cr	£
Balance b/d	35,000		

Accumulated depreciation

Dr	£	Cr	£
		Balance b/d	70,000

b) The business sold office equipment which had originally cost £8,500. The sale proceeds were £3,250. The accumulated depreciation was £5,100. Calculate the profit or loss on disposal. (3 marks)

	Profit	Loss
£		

c) Complete the following table by ticking the true or false box beside each option. (2 marks)

	True	False
Depreciation charges are transferred to the statement of profit or loss at the end of the year.		
Accumulated depreciation is a debit in the extended trial balance.		
Depreciation is an example of the accruals concept.		

Task 3 (19 marks)

This task is about ledger accounting, including accruals and prepayments, and applying ethical principles.

a) Enter the figures below into the appropriate trial balance columns. Do not enter zeros in empty cells and do not use negative numbers. (2 marks)

Extract from the trial balance

Account	Ledger balance £	Dr £	Cr £
Prepaid expenses	660		
Discounts received	230		
Prepaid income	1,200		
Carriage inwards	835		
Discounts allowed	875		

b) You are working on the accounting records of a business with the year-end 31 March 2021.

You can ignore VAT.

The business applies the accruals concept.

You are looking at the admin expenses for the year.

There is an opening balance of £300 which represents a prepayment of admin expenses on 31 March 2020.

The cash book shows payments of admin expenses during the year of £3,640.

This includes the following payments.

Details	Dates	Amount £
Office equipment rental	1 January 2021 to 31 December 2021	2,400
Telephone expenses	Quarter ended 30 April 2021	270

Calculate the value of the adjustment required to the admin expenses account on 31 March 2021. (3 marks)

£ 1,590

c) Using the figures from b), complete the admin expenses account below, clearly showing the amount to transfer to the statement of profit or loss. (6 marks)

Admin expenses

Dr	£	Cr	£

d) Rent income for the year shows an opening accrual of £500.

The cashbook shows receipts of rent income for the year of £50,000.

Rent income of £2,000 for the month of March 2021 was received on 15 April 2021.

Calculate the rent income for the year by completing the table below. (6 marks)

Use minus signs to show a deduction from the cashbook figure.

	£
Cashbook figure	50,000
Opening adjustment	
Closing adjustment	
Rent income for the year	

e) Your sales manager has asked you to explain why you have included the rent income received on 15 April 2021 as this was after the year-end. Which one of the following is an acceptable explanation? (2 marks)

	Acceptable reason	Not acceptable reason
This is an expense which relates to the year ended 31 March 2021.		
We want to reduce the income for the following year.		
This is an income that was earned in the year ended 31 March 2021.		

Task 4 (20 marks)

This task is about accounting for adjustments.

You are a trainee accountant in an accounting practice, and you are working on the accounts of a business with the year end of 31 March 2021.

A trial balance has been drawn up and a suspense account opened.

a) You have been asked to make some adjustments and corrections. (14 marks)

You can ignore VAT.

- The allowance for doubtful debt needs to be adjusted to 2% of the trade receivables. Calculate the value of the adjustment and enter this into the extract of the trial balance below.

- An admin expense of £56 has been posted as £65.

- A payment of £300 was received from a credit customer. The correct debit entry was made. No other entries were made.

- Motor expenses of £80 have been incorrectly posted to rent expenses.

Extract from the extended trial balance

Ledger account	Ledger Balances		Adjustments	
	Dr £	Cr £	Dr £	Cr£
Allowance for doubtful debts		380		
Allowance for doubtful debts -adjustment				
Admin expenses	1,640			
Bank	8,750			
Depreciation charges	1,200			
Equipment at cost	65,000			
Equipment – accumulated depreciation		14,000		
Irrecoverable debts	150			
Purchases	58,000			
Purchase ledger control account		4,870		
Prepaid expenses	230			
Motor expenses	7,500			
Rent expenses	6080			
Sales ledger control account	42,000			
Suspense account	309			

b) Show the entries to close off the admin expenses account at the end of the year. (4 marks)

	Dr £	Cr £

c) You have been asked by your manager to finalise the limited company accounts for an important client. You have not been trained in the completion of company accounts and do not think that you can complete this accurately. What do you do? (2 marks)

Complete the work to the best of your ability, as this will keep your manager happy.	
Explain to your manager that you are not competent to complete this work and ask that a more experienced colleague complete the task.	
Ignore the request and keep quiet, hoping that it will all go away.	

Task 5 (23 marks)

This task is about period end routines, using accounting records, and the extended trial balance.

You are preparing the bank reconciliation for a business at the 31 March 2021. The bank statement and cash book do not agree. The bank statement has been compared with the cash book and the following points noted.

1	Bank charges of £56 are showing on the bank statement but have not yet been entered into the cash book.
2	A cheque payment of £3,400 has been entered into the accounting records but is not yet showing on the bank statement.
3	A BACS receipt from a credit customer for £600 is showing on the bank statement but no journal entry has been made for this.
4	A payment received from a credit customer of £300 has been entered in the cash book, but this is not yet showing on the bank statement.
5	A standing order for rent of £440 has been entered in the cash book as £404.
6	A bank payment of £200 for office supplies has been entered into the accounting records but is not yet showing on the bank statement.

a) Use the table below to show the **THREE** adjustments that need to be made to the cash book. Do not enter zeros and do not use negative numbers. (6 marks)

Adjustment	Dr £	Cr £

b) Which two of the following statement are true? (3 marks)

A suspense account should have a balance of zero once all the necessary adjustments have been made.	
The wages control account includes a list of all employees.	
The irrecoverable debts account is a summary of balances which will be paid in the next financial year.	
The sales ledger control account gives a summary of the amount of money owed to a business by its customers.	
A prepaid expense is an amount that has not been paid by the business at the end of the financial year.	

c) You are working on the accounts of a different business with the year end of 31 March 2021.

You have been given the following extended trial balance. All necessary adjustments have been made.

Extend the figures to the appropriate statement in the extended trial balance on the next page.

Do not enter zeros in unused cells.

(14 marks)

Ledger account	Ledger balances		Adjustments		Statement of profit or loss		Statement of financial position	
	Dr £	Cr £	Dr £	Cr £	Dr £	Cr £	Dr £	Cr £
Accruals		550						
Allowance for doubtful debt		300	50					
Doubtful debt adjustment				50				
Bank	38,000							
Capital		20,000						
Closing inventory			3,200	3,200				
Depreciation charges			4,400					
Equipment at cost	128,000							
Equipment – acc. depreciation		22,000		4,400				
Irrecoverable debts			99					
Office expenses	3,600			600				
Opening inventory	2,800							
Prepayments			600					
Purchases	87,190		1,260					
Purchase ledger control account		8,000						
Sales		213,000		300				
Sales ledger control account	12,000			99				
Suspense	960		300	1,260				
VAT		8,700						
Profit / Loss for the year								
Totals	272,550	272,550	9,909	9,909				

Answers

Answers are shown in bold.

Workings and explanations are included to help you understand the answers and these are shown at the end of each task.

Task 1 (21 marks)

This task is about non-current assets.

You are working on the accounting records of TC Enterprises for the year ended 31 March 2021.

You can ignore VAT in this task.

The following is an extract from a purchase invoice for some office equipment purchased by TC Enterprises.

Alphabeta Office Supplies Ltd 16 The Terrace Northport		30 September 2020
To: TC Enterprises		
Item	Details	Total cost £
Corner desk unit	DK101A	560.00
Assembly cost	DK101A	60.00
Manager's chair	MC20B	220.00
Net total		840.00

Payment was made by bank transfer on 30 September 2020.

The following relates to the sale of a vehicle.

Item description	Transport lorry ID no. TPL12
Date of sale	1 June 2020
Selling price	£8,000

The business has a policy of capitalising equipment over £500.

Vehicles are depreciated at 20% diminishing balance. This depreciation is charged in the year of acquisition but none in the year of disposal.

Office equipment is depreciated at 10% straight line assuming no residual value and charged in equal instalments for each month the asset is owned.

a) For the year ended 31 March 2021, record the following in the extract from the non-current assets register below. (18 marks)

Any acquisition of new equipment.
Any disposals of equipment.
Depreciation.

Note. Not every cell will require an answer. Round your answers to the nearest whole pound. Use the date format DD/MM/YY for your answers.

Extract from the non-current assets register.

Description	Acquisition date	Cost £	Depreciation charges £	Carrying amount £	Funding method	Disposal proceeds £	Disposal date
Office equipment							
Meeting table	01/06/19	1,200			Bank		
Year-end 31/03/20			100	1,100			
Year-end 31/03/21			120	980			
Corner desk unit	30/09/20	620			Bank		
Year-end 31/03/21			31	589			
Vehicles							
Delivery van DV62	01/04/18	30,000			Loan		
Year-end 31/03/19			6,000	24,000			
Year-end 31/03/20			4,800	19,200			
Year-end 31/03/21			3,840	15,360			
Transport lorry TPL12	01/04/18	80,000			Credit		
Year-end 31/03/19			16,000	64,000			
Year-end 31/03/20			12,800	51,200			
Year-end 31/03/21			0	0		8,000	01/06/20

Workings and explanations:

The meeting table was an existing item and is depreciated at 10% for a whole year. £1,200 x 10% = £120. The carrying amount is the cost less the accumulated depreciation. £1,100 - £120 = £980.

The corner desk was the new acquisition and was purchased for £620. This includes the desk and the cost of assembly. £560 + £60 = £620. The funding method was from the bank. The depreciation was calculated at 10% per annum, then separated into months. The depreciation method is straight line based on the months of ownership. It was purchased on 30 September 2020, so was owned from 1 October 2020 to 31 March 2021 = 6 months. £620 x 10% = £62. £62 divided by 12 months and multiplied by 6 months equals £31. The carrying amount is £620 - £31 = £589.

The manager's chair is not capitalised as an asset because it is under £500, which is the policy for this business. (This would be posted to office expenses instead).

The delivery van was an existing asset and was depreciated at 20% diminishing balance. Carrying amount x 20 %. £19,200 x 20% = £3,840. The carrying amount is £19,200 - £3,840 = £15,360.

The transport lorry was disposed of in the year so the disposal proceeds of £8,000 and the date are entered in the non-current asset register. There is no depreciation charge as this is charged in the year of acquisition and not in the year of disposal. There is no carrying amount as the vehicle is no longer owned by the business.

b) The asset register should be checked against a physical count of assets at the end of the year. (3 marks)

True	√
False	

Explanation

A physical check on the assets is needed to ensure that the asset register is up to date. Occasionally items may have been disposed of during the year because they were broken, and the information not passed on to the accounts team.

Task 2 (19 marks)

This task is about ledger accounting for non-current assets.

You are working on the accounting records of a business with the year end of 31 March 2021.

VAT can be ignored.

A new vehicle has been acquired and it is expected to have a useful life of 5 years.

The cost was £26,000 and this was paid from the bank.

The business plans to sell the vehicle after 5 years when it is expected to have a residual value of £5,000.

Vehicles are depreciated using the straight-line method with a full year's depreciation in the year of acquisition and none in the year of disposal.

Depreciation has already been entered in the accounting records for other vehicles.

a) Calculate the depreciation charge for the new vehicle. (12 marks)

| £ 4,200 |

Workings:

Cost less residual value, divided by years of useful life.
£26,000 - £5,000 = £21,000 / 5 years = £4,200.

Make entries for the acquisition of the new vehicle and the depreciation charge of the new vehicle.

Balance off the accounts clearly showing the amount to be transferred to the Statement of Profit or Loss or carried down.

Vehicles at cost

Dr	£	Cr	£
Balance b/d	260,000	**Bal c/d**	**286,000**
Bank	**26,000**		
	286,000		286,000

Depreciation charges

Dr	£	Cr	£
Balance b/d	35,000	**Transfer to SoPL**	**39,200**
Accumulated depreciation	**4,200**		
	39,200		39,200

Accumulated depreciation

Dr	£	Cr	£
Bal c/d	**74,200**	Balance b/d	70,000
		Depreciation charges	**4,200**
	74,200		74,200

Workings and explanation:

The purchase of the new vehicle was made by the bank. Debit vehicles account as increasing the asset. Credit bank (not shown in this question) as decreasing the asset or bank balance.

Depreciation charges are an expense, so these are entered as a debit with the narrative accumulated depreciation. The account is balanced and transferred to the statement of profit or loss.

Accumulated depreciation is credited with the depreciation charges. Accumulated depreciation is carried forward with the asset until it is disposed of.

b) The business sold office equipment which has originally cost £8,500. The sale proceeds were £3,250. The accumulated depreciation was £5,100. Calculate the profit or loss on disposal. (3 marks)

	Profit	Loss
£150		√

Workings and explanation:

Always best to draw up the disposal account for this type of question.

Disposals

Dr	£	Cr	£
Office equipment	8,500	Bank (sale proceeds)	3,250
		Accumulated depreciation	5,100
		Loss on disposal (to SoPL)	150
	8,500		8,500

This is a loss because it is a credit in the disposal account and a debit in the statement of profit and loss, indicating an expense.

c) Complete the following table by ticking the true or false box beside each option. (2 marks)

	True	False
Depreciation charges are transferred to the statement of profit or loss at the end of the year.	√	
Accumulated depreciation is a debit in the extended trial balance.		√
Depreciation is an example of the accruals concept.	√	

Explanation:

Depreciation charges are an expense, and these are transferred to the statement of profit or loss at the end of the year.

Accumulated depreciation is a credit in the extended trial balance. Remember that it is always on the opposite site to the asset.

Depreciation is an example of the accruals concept because the accruals concept requires us to match the expense to the period in which it was incurred. The value of the asset is gradually spread over the asset life, matching it to the periods in which it is used.

Task 3 (21 marks)

This task is about ledger accounting, including accruals and prepayments, and applying ethical principles.

a) Enter the figures below into the appropriate trial balance columns. Do not enter zeros in empty cells and do not use negative numbers. (2 marks)

Extract from the trial balance

Account	Ledger balance £	Dr £	Cr £
Prepaid expenses	660	**660**	
Discounts received	230		**230**
Prepaid income	1,200		**1,200**
Carriage inwards	835	**835**	
Discounts allowed	875	**875**	

Explanations:

Prepaid expenses are money paid in advance, so these are an asset to the business.
Discounts received are a form of income, and income is a credit.
Prepaid income is money paid in advance by customers and is owed back to the customers, so this is a liability. Liabilities are credits.
Carriage inwards is the 'postage and packing' costs of buying something and this is an expense to the business. Expenses are debits.

Discounts allowed are discounts given to customers and these cost the business money, so are expense to the business. Expenses are debits.

b) You are working on the accounting records of a business with the year-end 31 March 2021.

You can ignore VAT.

The business applies the accruals concept.

You are looking at the admin expenses for the year.

There is an opening balance of £300 which represents a prepayment of admin expenses on 31 March 2020.

The cash book shows payments of admin expenses during the year of £3,640.

This includes the following payments.

Details	Dates	Amount £
Office equipment rental	1 January 2021 to 31 December 2021	2,400
Telephone expenses	Quarter ended 30 April 2021	270

Calculate the value of the adjustment required to the admin expenses account on 31 March 2021. (3 marks)

£1,890

Workings and Explanation:

Office equipment rental of £2,400 was paid for the period of 1 January to 31 December 2021, 12 months.
The year ended on 31 March 2021.
The period from 1 April to 31 December 2021 has been paid in advance, a prepaid expense.
£2,400 / 12 months = £200 per month.
April – December = 9 months.
£200 x 9 months = £1,800 prepaid.

Telephone expenses of £270 for the quarter ended 30 April 2021 were paid. This covered the months of February, March and April 2021.
The year ended 31 March 2021, so April is prepaid.
£270 / 3 months = £90 prepaid.

Add the two prepayments together for the value of the adjustment.

£1,800 + £90 = £1,890

c) Using the figures from b), complete the admin expenses account below, clearly showing the amount to transfer to the statement of profit or loss. (6 marks)

Admin expenses

Dr	£	Cr	£
Reversal of prepaid expenses	300	**Prepaid expenses**	1,890
Bank	3,640	Transfer to SoPL	2,050
	3,940		3,940

Explanations:

The reversal was made by crediting the prepaid expenses account and debiting the admin expenses account. This is because the prepaid expenses was a debit at the end of the previous year and we are 'bringing it down' into the current year.

The bank is a debit because this money was paid from the bank and so the bank was credited (reducing the balance).

The prepaid expenses are credited to the admin expenses account and debited to the prepaid expenses account. Remember that prepaid expenses are an asset at the end of the year, therefore a debit entry.

d) Rent income for the year shows an opening accrual of £500.
The cash book shows receipts of rent income for the year of £50,000.
Rent income of £2,000 for the month of March 2021 was received on 15 April 2021.
Calculate the rent income for the year by completing the table below. (6 marks)

Use minus signs to show a deduction from the cashbook figure.

	£
Cashbook figure	50,000
Opening adjustment	-500
Closing adjustment	2,000
Rent income for the year	51,500

Workings and Explanation:

It is always a good idea to draw up the T account for this type of question as it will help you to check your answers.

Rent income

Dr	£	Cr	£
Reversal of accrued income	500	Bank	50,000
Transfer to SoPL	51,500	Accrued income	2,000
	52,000		52,000

The accrued income was a debit, so we credit this out of the accrued income account and debit it into the rent income account. The bank balance was increased when the rent income was received so that was a debit. The entry in the rent income account is therefore a credit. The income for March of £2,000 was received after the year end but should be included in the year so this is credited to the income account and debited to the accrued income account. You can use the answers in the T account to complete the table or simply check the answers. Note that the transfer to the statement of profit or loss is the same in the T account as showing as the rent income for the year in the table.

e) Your sales manager has asked you to explain why you have included the rent income received on 15 April 2021 as this was after the year-end. Which <u>one</u> of the following is an acceptable explanation? (2 marks)

	Acceptable reason	Not acceptable reason
This is an expense which relates to the year ended 31 March 2021.		√
We want to reduce the income for the following year.		√
This is an income that was earned in the year ended 31 March 2021.	√	

Explanations:

This is not an expense; it is an income. Watch the words in this type of question.
We cannot move income to reduce it in the following year. It must go to the correct year.
This is an income that was earned in the year and therefore matched to the year it was earned and not when it was received.

Task 4 (20 marks)

This task is about accounting for adjustments.

a) You are a trainee accountant in an accounting practice, and you are working on the accounts of a business with the year end of 31 March 2021.

A trial balance has been drawn up and a suspense account opened.

You have been asked to make some adjustments and corrections. (14 marks)

You can ignore VAT.

- The allowance for doubtful debt needs to be adjusted to 2% of the trade receivables. Calculate the value of the adjustment and enter this into the extract of the trial balance below.

- An admin expense of £56 has been posted as £65.

- A payment of £300 was received from a credit customer. The correct debit entry was made. No other entries were made.

- Motor expenses of £80 have been incorrectly posted to rent expenses.

Extract from the extended trial balance

Ledger account	Ledger Balances		Adjustments	
	Dr £	Cr £	Dr £	Cr£
Allowance for doubtful debts		380		**460**
Allowance for doubtful debts -adjustment			**460**	
Admin expenses	1,640			9
Bank	8,750			
Depreciation charges	1,200			
Equipment at cost	65,000			
Equipment – accumulated depreciation		14,000		
Irrecoverable debts	150			
Purchases	58,000			
Purchase ledger control account		4,870		
Prepaid expenses	230			
Motor expenses	7,500		**80**	
Rent expenses	6080			80
Sales ledger control account	42,000			300
Suspense account	309		309	

Workings and Explanations:

The allowance for doubtful debt needs to be adjusted to 2% of the trade receivables. The trade receivable is the sales ledger control account. £42,000 x 2% = £840. The allowance for doubtful debt already has a balance of £380 so we need to adjust this up to £840. £840 - £380 = £460. We credit the allowance for doubtful debt with

£460 to increase the balance to £840. The debit entry goes to the allowance for doubtful debt adjustment account.

An admin expense of £56 has been posted as £65. This means that the admin expense account includes a figure of £65 instead of £56, a difference of £9. We need to reduce the admin expenses account by crediting it with £9. As there is no other error or account affected, the debit entry goes to the suspense account.

A payment of £300 was received from a credit customer. The correct debit entry was made. No other entries were made. If we think about what entries should have been made, we can see what has been done wrong. £300 from a credit customer should have been debited to the bank and credited to the sales ledger control account. The debit entry to the bank was correctly entered. The credit entry to the sales ledger control account is missing. We enter this and then post the debit entry to the suspense account as no other error or account is affected.

Note: The suspense account may need to be adjusted with more than one entry, so just add them together.

Motor expenses of £80 have been incorrectly posted to rent expenses. We need to move this from the rent expenses account and into the motor expenses account. We take it out of the rent expenses account by crediting it and then add it into the motor expenses account with a debit entry.

b) Show the entries to close off the admin expenses account at the end of the year. (4 marks)

	Dr £	Cr £
Statement of profit or loss	1,631	
Admin expenses		1,631

Explanation:

This question is just asking you to double-entry the admin expenses out of the trial balance at the end of the year and transfer it to the statement of profit or loss. The admin expenses are a debit in the extended trial balance, so you are crediting them out of there and debiting them into the SoPL. And don't forget this adjustment in this one!

c) You have been asked by your manager to finalise the limited company accounts for an important client. You have not been trained in the completion of company accounts and do not think that you can complete this accurately. What do you do? (2 marks)

Complete the work to the best of your ability, as this will keep your manager happy.	
Explain to your manager that you are not competent to complete this work and ask that a more experienced colleague complete the task.	✓
Ignore the request and keep quiet, hoping that it will all go away.	

Explanation:

You should never undertake work that you are not competent to complete as this will breach your fundamental ethical principle of professional competence and due care.

Task 5 (23 marks)

This task is about period end routines, using accounting records, and the extended trial balance.

You are preparing the bank reconciliation for a business at the 31 March 2021. The bank statement and cash book do not agree. The bank statement has been compared with the cash book and the following points noted.

1	Bank charges of £56 are showing on the bank statement but have not yet been entered into the cash book.
2	A cheque payment of £3,400 has been entered into the accounting records but is not yet showing on the bank statement.
3	A BACS receipt from a credit customer for £600 is showing on the bank statement but no journal entry has been made for this.
4	A payment received from a credit customer of £300 has been entered in the cash book, but this is not yet showing on the bank statement.
5	A standing order for rent of £440 has been entered in the cash book as £404.
6	A bank payment of £200 for office supplies has been entered into the accounting records but is not yet showing on the bank statement.

a) Use the table below to show the **THREE** adjustments that need to be made to the cash book. Do not enter zeros and do not use negative numbers. (6 marks)

Adjustment	Dr £	Cr £
1		56
3	600	
5		36

Explanations:

Adjustment 1: The bank charges <u>have not been entered into the cash book.</u> Look for key words like this. It has not been entered, so this adjustment needs to be done. As they are bank charges, these reduce the bank balance, so the cash book is credited with the £56.

Adjustment 2: The payment <u>has been entered into the accounting records</u>, so this tells us that we do not need to make any adjustments in the cash book.

Adjustment 3: A BACS receipt from a customer is on the bank statement but <u>no journal entry has been made</u>. This tells us that we need to make the journal entry. As this is a receipt, it is increasing the balance, so this is a debit entry.

Adjustment 4: A payment from a customer <u>has been entered in the cash book</u>, so we do not need to do anything with this.

Adjustment 5: A standing order payment has been entered incorrectly in the cash book. £404 was entered when it should have been £440. We need to adjust the cash book with the difference. £440 - £404 = £36. The amount entered was lower than the amount of the payment, so we need to increase the payment by £36 by crediting the cash book.

Adjustment 6: A payment of £200 <u>has been entered into the accounting records</u>, so we do not need to do anything with this.

b) Which two of the following statement are true? (3 marks)

A suspense account should have a balance of zero once all the necessary adjustments have been made.	√
The wages control account includes a list of all employees.	
The irrecoverable debts account is a summary of balances which will be paid in the next financial year.	
The sales ledger control account gives a summary of the amount of money owed to a business by its customers.	√
A prepaid expense is an amount that has not been paid by the business at the end of the financial year.	

Explanations:

A suspense account is used in the initial trial balance to account for any errors or missing entries. This must be cleared before the extended trial balance is drawn up.

The sales ledger control account is a total of all the money owed by the customers to the business. It is also known as the trade receivables account.

c) You are working on the accounts of a different business with the year end of 31 March 2021.

You have been given the following extended trial balance. All necessary adjustments have been made.

Extend the figures to the appropriate statement in the extended trial balance on the next page. (14 marks)

Do not enter zeros in unused cells.

Ledger account	Ledger balances		Adjustments		Statement of profit or loss		Statement of financial position	
	Dr £	Cr £	Dr £	Cr £	Dr £	Cr £	Dr £	Cr £
Accruals		550						550
Allowance for doubtful debt		300	50					250
Doubtful debt adjustment				50	50			
Bank	38,000						38,000	
Capital		20,000						20,000
Closing inventory			3,200	3,200		3,200	3,200	
Depreciation charges			4,400		4,400			
Equipment at cost	128,000						128,000	
Equipment – acc. depreciation		22,000		4,400				26,400
Irrecoverable debts			99		99			
Office expenses	3,600			600	3,000			
Opening inventory	2,800				2,800			
Prepayments			600				600	
Purchases	87,190		1,260		88,450			
Purchase ledger control account		8,000						8,000
Sales		213,000		300		213,300		
Sales ledger control account	12,000			99			11,901	
Suspense	960		300	1,260				
VAT		8,700						8,700
Profit / Loss for the year					117,801			117,801
Totals	272,550	272,550	9,909	9,909	216,550	216,550	181,701	181701

45

Explanations:

Use EIAL at the top of your headings like this:

SoPL   SoFP
Dr   Cr   Dr   Cr
E   I   A   L

Now you will be able to follow the explanations easier.

Accruals are a liability for the business. Remember accrual means owed.

Allowance for doubtful debt is the provision for a liability.

Doubtful debt adjustment can be a debit or credit entry in the SoPL as this is either increasing or decreasing the expense.

Bank could be an asset or liability depending on whether it is in funds or overdrawn. This one is a debit balance, so it is an asset.

Capital is a liability to the business as it is owed back to the owner.

Closing inventory is an asset in the SoFP because it is something that the business owns. It is a 'reverse' expense in the SoPL because it is deducted from the cost of sales.

Depreciation charges are an expense to the business.

Equipment at cost is something that the business owns so this is an asset.

Accumulated depreciation reduces the value of the asset, so this is a liability against the equipment so a credit entry. It will always be on the opposite side to the asset.

Irrecoverable debts are money that the business will not be receiving from its credit customers, so this is an expense to the business.

Offices expenses are expenses.

Opening inventory was stock on the shelves at the beginning of the year which has been used or sold, so this is an expense.

Prepayments are prepaid expenses, so these are an asset to the business.

Purchases are items bought for resale, so these are an expense.

Purchase ledger control account is the trade payables account, so this is a <u>liability</u> as it is money that the business owes to its suppliers.

Sales are a form of <u>income.</u>

Sales ledger control account is the trade receivables account, so this is an <u>asset</u> as it is money that the business is owed by its customers.

Suspense account should be clear if adjustments have been correctly made.

VAT could be a debit or credit. In this case it is a credit, so this is money that the business owes to HMRC, so a <u>liability.</u>

The profit/loss for the year is calculated by finding the difference between the debit and credit columns of the statement of profit or loss. The same figure should be the difference between the debit and credit columns of the statement of financial position.

Marks sheet:

Task	Available marks	Your marks - first attempt	Your marks – second attempt	Notes
1a	18			
1b	3			
2a	12			
2b	3			
2c	2			
3a	2			
3b	3			
3c	6			
3d	6			
3e	2			
4a	14			
4b	4			
4c	2			
5a	6			
5b	3			
5c	14			
Total	100			

Printed in Great Britain
by Amazon